IMAGINE. BUILD. PLAY.

Rescue Mission with My STEM Invention

Inspiring Story for 6-12 Year Old Kids, Who Love to Imagine, Build and Play.

Written by:
Sumita Mukherjee

wizkidsclub.com

More books from WIZKIDS CLUB:

Stem/Steam Activity Books: 6-10 Year Kids $6.99 Each

COOL SCIENCE EXPERIMENTS FOR KIDS

Grades: 1-5
Skill level: Beginner
Time: 19 projects; 30-40 minutes each

COOL SCIENCE EXPERIMENTS FOR KIDS is an amazing book full of hands-on activities. With awesome Science, Technology, Engineering, Art and Math project ideas, it is an easy way to entertain any bored kid! A great way to acquire 21st century skills and STEM learning.

Inside this book you will find projects on Simple Machines, Merry-go Round, Spinning Doll, Exploding Bottle, Safe Slime, Architecture, Crafts, Games and more!

Loads of fun with projects that burst, glow, erupt, spin, run, tick and grow!

FAMOUS STEM INVENTORS

Grades: 1-5
Skill level: Beginner
Time: Reading time: 15-20 mins and activities of 20-30 minutes each.

FAMOUS STEM INVENTORS introduces kids to the world's most famous young inventors in the field of S.T.E.M (Science, Technology, Engineering and Math). All things that we enjoy are a product of brilliant minds, scientists and engineers. This book imparts information that is interesting and engaging to young boys and girls between 6-10 years of age.

STORY OF INVENTORS: Kids will be transported to the fascinating world of famous creators and learn about their first inventions: Glowing paper, Popsicle, Windsurf board, Television, Earmuffs and more. The book arouses their natural curiosity to be inspired from their role models.

DESIGN PROCESS: It showcases the Engineering Design Process behind every invention. Highlights what they invented and how they invented, thereby, revealing the steps to all new discoveries.

SKETCHING AND DESIGNING ACTIVITY: It encourages kids to sketch and design their own ideas through the design activity. This book prompts kids to think creatively and it arouses their natural curiosity to build, make and tinker.

STEAM AHEAD! DIY FOR KIDS

Grades: 1-5
Skill level: Beginner
Time: 21 projects; 30-40 minutes each

STEAM AHEAD! DIY FOR KIDS is an amazing book full of hands-on activities. With awesome Science, Technology, Engineering, Art and Math project ideas, it is an easy way to entertain any bored kid! A great way to acquire 21st century skills and STEM learning.

Inside this book you will find projects on LED cards, dance pads, handmade soaps, bubble blowers, Play-Doh circuits, cloud lanterns, scribbling bots and more!

Awarded 5 stars by READERS' FAVORITE site, Parents, Educators, Bloggers and Homeschoolers.

Rescue Mission with My STEM Invention

JOIN THE WIZKIDS CLUB TEAM!

The WIZKIDS CLUB features Highly Engaging Activities, Experiments, DIYs, Travel Stories, Science Experiment Books and more!

Visit www.wizkidsclub.com today!

IMAGINE. BUILD. PLAY.

www.wizkidsclub.com

Author: Sumita Mukherjee

Designer: Lester D. Basubas

First Edition: May 2018

All rights reserved@Sumita Mukherjee 2018

TABLE OF CONTENTS

ABOUT THE BOOK:

Join the global initiative of raising the next generation of creative leaders, engineers and scientists. Thousands of kids are being catapulted into the magical world of S.T.E.M (Science, Technology, Engineer and Math).

This book is ideal for kids who are creative thinkers and problem solvers. Through the story of the STEM enthusiastic kids, get inspired to look at real world problem and find solutions. It is thinking outside the box and scientific progress that can save the day.

ABOUT THE AUTHOR:

Sumita Mukherjee is a NASA STEM certified leader and bestselling children's book author. Her books are to inspire young readers to develop a love for discovery and learn about the world around them.

The series of STEAM (Science, Technology, Engineering, Art and Math) and STEM books encourages kids to invent and explore, to empower themselves and see themselves as world leaders and problem solvers. Her books celebrate diversity, spark curiosity and capture children's imaginations!

Her website, WizKidsclub.com was created with a vision to raise the next generation of creative leaders. WizKidsclub offers STEAM programs, educational books, hands-on projects, DIYs, travel stories and engineering books perfect for children 4-12 years.

 Rescue Mission with My STEM Invention

CHAPTER 1: School Tech Contest

"Well, kids, it's almost end of term. That means it's time for the "BEST TECH IDEA" contest!" Mrs Smith, our science teacher said with twinkling eyes and a huge smile on her face. "There is no limit to what you can create, let your imagination run free!"

For an ex NASA scientist, Mrs Smith seemed really excited about a high school science contest. She'd won a high school science competition where the prize was a scholarship to MIT. After graduation, she'd gone to work at NASA which is a really cool background for a school teacher.

"Last year the Frankie twins surprised us with the Forever slime soap! I am still using it and I think it will last me a life time..." Mrs Smith chuckled.

Nicole, my best friend nudged me from behind. "Ugh! The Frankie twins must have hacked someone else's idea, it's impossible that they could create a soap that lasts forever! That idea DID NOT come from their mini brains!" Narrowing her dark eyes, she tossed the curly black lock that dared to fall in front of her eyes, her cocoa skin flushed.

Nicole is the best chemist in school and loves whipping up unique brews. Last year she invented a color changing cake liquid. She's simply unbeatable when it comes to devising potions. "Come on, we have to do something really great this time...we must beat the Frankie twins!" I replied with a strong voice, staring firmly at Nicole.

"How about making a 'Lie Detector' to catch the twins out?" Alan, sitting next to Nicole, suggested. "Can you imagine their faces when we expose them as cheats?!" he chuckled, rubbing the end of his pencil against his nose.

"Tiffany...have you come up with an idea?" Mrs. Smith interrupted, noticing that our giggling trio was not paying attention. She stared sternly at me through her steel-rimmed round glasses.

"There are so many possibilities, we are struggling to pick the winning one!" I said confidently, sitting up straight. Out of the corner of my eye I saw the Frankie twins whispering to each other.

The Frankie twins are two super sly, sneaky girls. They eavesdrop on other people's conversation and spread gossip around school. They are a pair of goody two-shoes without an original thought between them.

We've been arch-enemies since that day in the library. I'd spent hours reading and making notes for an assignment, then caught them photographing my work with their mobile phone to pass it off as their own. Nicole and I are both smart and work hard. We usually alternate first and second positions in class. But when those two ditsy, freckled Frankies get A's for copying others' work, it makes me mad.

Saved by the ringing bell, Mrs Smith took her eyes off me and announced "OK, class, you are free to go. The contest is in five days time, may the best IDEA win! Have a good after..." That was all I heard. I was up out of my seat and through the door before she finished her sentence, Alan and Nicole at my heels.

I stopped them, "Alan, do you have any ideas?" I asked. Alan is short, skinny and constantly scratching himself. Eczema. But, he is a whiz with computers and spends his weekends inventing new mobile apps. One day, he says, Apple will buy one of his developments. He is busy trying to develop a technology that recycles polluted air, converting it into fresh oxygen. It wasn't going well.

Anxiously, Alan scratched his scalp. "I was thinking we could build something like a Spy Pen?" he suggested.

"Nah, the Frankie's made a Spy Pen two years ago. We need something really different, something dynamic to wow the judges. Otherwise, those conniving nitwits will win the contest again." I said.

"We'll need help if we want to win this year, any ideas who to ask?" Nicole asked.

"Us!" a squeaky voice interjected, "We'll help you, losers!"

Cackling like witches, the Frankie twins strolled past us. They'd been listening in on our conversation.

"Forget them," I pulled Nicole's sleeve. I could see she was about to give them a nasty piece of her mind. "Let's get out of here. Alan, are you coming?"

"Oh, yes, yes, I'm with you," he gasped, jogging to catch up with us as he tightened the straps on his enormous backpack.

The three of us marched through the main door. There was no way that I was going to let the Science Contest Trophy slip through my fingers again. I still smarted at the memory of last year's awards ceremony.

Confident that our entry, the color changing cake liquid, was a winner, Nicole and I were flabbergasted when the red-headed rats unveiled their 'Forever Slime Soap' as the entries closed. The sly twosome told everyone they were working on an app then produced something different. Although it was the winning entry, none of us believe it was their original work. Our invention raised over $100 for charity but that was poor consolation for being losers!

"Let's go to my house, we can brainstorm some ideas. My dad is at home today, he may have some suggestions," I said.

We unlocked our bikes and began peddling home. "Beat ya both," I challenged, standing up on my peddles and putting all my frustration into cycling fast. We barely noticed the route home due to the thoughts and ideas jostling in our heads. Palm fronds high above our heads rattled in the stiff sea breeze, urging us faster.

At home, we leapt off our bikes, leaving them on the green front lawn in front of the white stucco bungalow. Grabbing our backpacks, we barged through the front door.

"Dad!" I yelled, "Dad, are you here?"

CHAPTER 2: Look Out for Oil Spills!

Next thing I knew, I was flat on my back. I'd dropped my bike and dashed inside so quickly, Bailey, my Golden Retriever didn't have time to play our usual welcome game on the front lawn, a big leap into my arms and some slopface. Bailey wasn't to be denied, however, and made sure he greeted me properly.

"Ohh buddy..." I laughed "Who's a good boy huh?"

My stomach growled. "Come on guys, let's have a snack and then we can think about our great invention." I called.

"I'm game!" Alan cheered, dropping his heavy backpack.

Despite his bony exterior, Alan was a big food fan. When he wasn't tinkering with his computer, he'd spend hours in the kitchen inventing new food combinations. Right now he was working on a range of vegetable flavored icecream, which he is convinced will be a winner. Not something I'll be investing in, however.

"I'll make broccoli muffins. I tried it at home and it was yummy – and healthy!" Nicole clapped her hands and buzzed off to the kitchen. Alan and I followed, hunger pangs gurgling.

What the three of us were really hoping for was a few rounds of my mom's world famous sandwiches. Crusty fresh bread, Emmenthal cheese, slices of home-grown juicy tomato sprinkled with fresh basil from mom's herb garden and topped with lime mayonnaise. Delicious!

Dad walked through into the kitchen, a big frown on his face. "What's wrong?" Mom asked. "The oil tanker Swan Majesty has run aground on the English coast and lost around 70,000 tons of her crude oil cargo. Unfortunately, it's a comparatively light oil, giving out its most harmful toxins into the water and air within a short time. The toxins are then carried up the food chain with deadly effect."

"The Grey seals living on that part of the coast and many seabirds have already died as a result of the disaster. One of only seven colonies of Green Rockpool starfish lives in that area and is now under threat. There is no way to clean up the oil spill fast enough to prevent any further damage," Dad sighed.

A Marine Biologist, Dad watches out for the health of the ocean and all the creatures that inhabit it or are reliant on it. He is often sent out to advise on methods to clean up marine areas after a disaster, or to help revive a destroyed reef.

"Oil spill...hmmm," Alan murmured thoughtfully. "Oh, I KNOW!"

"Are you thinking what I am thinking?" Nicole asked him, her eyes glued to his face.

"Maybe, if you are thinking of a machine that can cleanup the oil spill," Alan grinned.

"Well, we are trying all these things, but it is a slow process," Dad explained.

"How about bringing in ships and floating a series of pipes with huge pumps? It can start sucking the oil floating on top of the water?" I said. "Then they could clear the oil and water in the tanks."

"Hmm, that sounds like a possible solution," Dad replied thoughtfully.

"I'll check it out!" Alan grabbed his backpack, opening it and releasing all the 'secret treasures' he always carried around with him. A tangle of wires, sound kits, tubes and a laptop lay on the kitchen table. We stared at the pile, our food forgotten, while Alan booted up his laptop.

Dad stood up, "I'll leave you guys to do more research and come up with some ideas," and went back to his laptop.

"I need to run an errand, I won't be long. Have fun baking the muffins while I'm gone," Mom said as she picked up her bag and car keys, leaving us at the kitchen table.

"What if we can create a sponge-like substance that can absorb the oil and become solid? Or a powder that can stick to the oil and become hard…" I thought aloud.

"Like this?"Nicole asked. Alan and I looked up. She'd opened up my beanbag, extracted a handful of filler and dropped the tiny polystyrene balls into her glass of soda. The balls floated, making a carpet across the top of the liquid. "Yes!" I exclaimed. "What if we can create a polymer that adsorbs oil to become solid?"

Alan picked up our 'Invention Book' and turned to a fresh new page. In bold letters,he wrote across the top, "Oil-less Tech Sponge Idea".

"Time to go down to my basement lab," I decided. "We've only got five days to crack this idea."

CHAPTER 3: Sabotage

We tinkered and tweaked all weekend, convinced we were onto a winning idea. Nicole sat hunched over her microscope and test tubes. Wifts of smoke wafted up every now and then with the occasional nasty smell.

"Phew," I complained when a particularly noxious odour hit my nose. "What IS that?"

"One of my secret ingredients," Nicole answered. "If this works the way I hope it will, I'll tell you. Otherwise, I'll try my next idea." Nicole is not one to give up easily. I went back to my cutting and taping. I was trying to create a dredger that can suck up oil.

Alan lifting his eyes from the laptop asked, "What's this?" Holding the rectangular block covered in plastic tubes, somewhat resembling a hedgehog.

"Err… This is it," I explained. "It's a type of dredger. At the front, it spews the polymer balls over the oil. At the back, those tubes suck up the solid waste that is formed as the chemicals in the polymer balls react with the crude oil."

Alan sat taking notes and writing formulas down. It looked as though we'd had a snowstorm in the basement, the floor was covered with the beanbag filling. "Look," Nicole laughed, "snow in California!"

By the time Mom called us for dinner at 6pm on Sunday night, we were mighty pleased with ourselves. "We are absolutely ready for Presentation Day tomorrow," I declared. "A good night's sleep is in order, we have to be on top of our game in the morning to show those Frankie twins what REAL science is!"

I took particular care with my hair and outfit before leaving for school on Monday. Presentation Day calls for, well, my best personal presentation as well. When I got to school, I noticed that Alan had spruced himself up and Nicola had put a bunch of colorful ribbons in her hair.

Putting the invention book safely on my desk, we went into the hallway to check the presentation schedule. "Oh boy!" I said, "The Frankie duo are first."

"So what?" Nicole asked. "That will give our presentation more impact after seeing whatever pathetic effort they have devised."

Alan went to fetch the invention book. He returned looking troubled. "What's up?" I asked.

"I'm sure we left the book closed, but it was lying open and the Oiless Tech-Sponge page is rather crumpled," he said.

"I'm sure everything is OK," Nicole remarked. "It's too late for anyone to change their presentation anyway. Let's find our seats and watch the Frightful Frankies."

We chose seats in the centre of the front row, the better to psyche out the twins who were about to unveil their idea.

Mrs Smith was smiling as she introduced Doris and Dolores Frankie and their amazing 'Oiless Tech-Sponge'.

Not a sound emerged from my team for several seconds. How? How did they do this? How COULD they do this? This is outrageous. But the thoughts remained locked inside as Alan, Nicole and myself struggled to comprehend the extent of our disaster. We were on next!

Nicole was crying quietly while Alan feverishly scratched at his arms. I rose and climbed the steps onto the stage. "M..M..Mrs Smith," I stuttered. "Those fiendish Frankies stole our work! The Oiless Tech-Sponge is OUR idea!" Mrs Smith stared, her eyes narrowing.

"That is a very serious accusation, Tiffany. Can you prove they stole your idea?"

"It's obvious!" I exploded, "they are way too stupid to come up with this on their own. We worked all weekend and now we have nothing to show you." At this, I broke down, sobbing.

"That's enough, Tiffany. I'm disappointed in you three. You are my brightest, most diligent students and I had high hopes for your entry. If you still wish to participate in the contest, you have an extension of 48 hours to get your entry in."

Stumbling off the stage, I picked up our invention book and dumbly followed Nicole and Alan out into the hall. The Frankie twins were highfiving and giggling, excited about their victory. "You thieving, cheating..." Alan roared, while Nicole and I held him back. "Prove it!" Doris dared us. "You have no proof. Looks like you'll be watching us receive first again this year, Tiffany."

CHAPTER 4: S.T.E.M Game on!

The three of us were sitting gloomily around the kitchen table when Dad came in looking sad.

"Another dolphin was trapped in the fishing nets and died. It's body was washed up on the shore," he said.

I was glad to have something other than the cheating Frankie twins to talk about. "Those poor dolphins, that's such a pity." I said. "How does it happen?" Nicole shivered.

"It's called dolphin bycatch and is a real threat to dolphins," Dad explained. "When fishermen drag their nets through the water, trawling for fish, the dolphins are often caught in the net. It's a very dangerous situation for these amazing creatures. If the dolphin can't get loose, it can drown."

"Oh no!" Nicole gasped. "That's awful," said Alan. "What can the fishermen do to keep it from happening?" I asked urgently. "Surely there is something we can do to help?"

"Those are excellent questions and our team is working on it," Dad answered. "We are busy researching ways to save them. The local fishermen are very eager to hear ideas to help protect the dolphins. Knowing that you kids are eager to help to find a solution is good news."

Mom, noticing how glum we all were, opened the refridgerator. In an effort to raise the mood around the table, she suggested that she make some sandwiches. "You three have worked hard and deserve a break and some fun," she said. "Off you go to the beach, I'll bring a picnic along for you."

Once we got to the beach, it was difficult to remain gloomy for long. We rented three buggies and zipped over the sand dunes, chasing each other around the palm trees. Eventually, tired out, we parked near the water's edge, watching the sunlight sparkle on the turquoise sea. The waves gently lapped against the shore. Palm fronds softly rattled in the breeze and the hot sun stroked our bare shoulders. It was a perfect day for the beach.

"Wow," Nicole said. "How can anyone be miserable right now?"

"I've got an idea," Alan grinned. "One I think you'll like."

"I'm all ears," I said.

"Coo-ee" Mom called, waving. Our picnic lunch had arrived.

"I was thinking about the dolphins. Maybe if the nets were made of different materials the dolphins could slip through them," Alan suggested as we started to set up the table. He put his heavy backpack down.

"What do you have in there? It looks so heavy," Nicole asked. "Ahh... just some emergency stuff. It's my "secret treasure chest," Alan answered, politely brushing off the question. Nicole and I cackled at his reply, sounding remarkably like the Frankie twins. "Alan, you are such a dork!" I exclaimed.

"That's not a nice thing to say," I heard Mom's voice behind me.

She had arrived with a tray full of sandwiches. Bailey was with her, scampering around her feet. He knew she had some delicious food and he wanted some! "Bailey, stop it!"she said, "you'll trip me up." Bailey calmed down for a few seconds then, without warning he began to bark furiously.

We looked up and gasped. Our friend Noah was driving over the sand dunes on his red superbuggy - but he was out of control. The buggy zoomed left and right, skidding wildly across the sand. Then, it careened straight towards us!

"Whoa, whoa - look out!" Noah yelled, waving his hand.

We jumped out of the way in the nick of time.

BAM!

Rescue Mission with My STEM Invention

Noah crashed right into the table. The buggy tipped over into a channel left by the retreating tide. He was flung from the driver's seat, flying in a big cartwheel over the sand before landing on his back. The vehicle lay down, its wheels spinning.

"Noah!" I cried. "Are you okay?"

Noah slowly sat up, rubbing his head. "Yeah, I'm all right. A turtle was crossing the road, and I had to swerve to avoid hitting him."

"I'm just glad nobody got hurt," Mom said, breathing a sigh of relief. "Including the turtle."

"It's a good thing Bailey barked and warned us just in time," Mom added.

"A warning," I said thoughtfully.

Nicole knew just what I meant. "With sound! An alarm on nets," she beamed.

Alan got it too. "That would warn the dolphins!"

"Great idea! We could use underwater speakers," Alan added.

"Bailey should get some credit," I said, "after all, without him barking we wouldn't have had any warning at all."

"We could call it Dolphin Woofs," Nicole suggested.

Bailey began jumping with excitement, woofing and grinning, delighted to be included as part of the invention.

"Perfect," I clapped.

"Thanks for the brilliant idea," Alan said. I blushed, "You're welcome. What is it I did again?" We laughed. "Eat up!" Nicole called impatiently. "We have to get back to the house and begin working on our contest entry."

Alan and I didn't hesitate. Grabbing a sandwich each, we jumped onto our buggies and headed back. "Sorry, Mom, can you pack the picnic up please? We have important thinking to do!" I pleaded. Mom laughed, "That's OK, will do."

It was time to get down to it. The game was on! The Dolphin Woofs had to be designed and completed by tomorrow, on Monday we had to present it to our class. It was time we showed them the power of S.T.E.M.

CHAPTER 5: The Big Reveal!

It was a quiet, nervous trio who stood outside the school hall the following day. We'd learned the hard way to guard our 'Book of Inventions' with our lives. Sick with nerves, none of us could bear to watch the Frankie twins this round.

Anna, one of our class mates who had a bit of a crush on Alan, slipped out of the hall as the twins left the stage. "They had nothing to show about their idea," she whispered. "They clearly don't know what it even means, let alone how to make it work!"

"Serves them right," Nicole growled. "What did the judges say?"

"Well, those girls can charm the birds out of the trees," Anna said. "They present themselves as slick and knowledgeable, but there is no science behind their presentation. Mrs Smith looks quite annoyed."

Surprisingly, this didn't ease any of our nervous tension. But our curiosity getting the better of us, we slipped into the hall and stood quietly in the shadows, hearts thudding. We wanted to see how the Frankie twins pulled their deceit off.

There the mean, freckly cheats stood under the spotlight, grinning confidently. "Please explain clearly what your first step is," Mrs Smith snapped. "I keep asking the question but I am not getting a proper answer from you."

The color rose in both of their faces. Doris squirmed uncomfortably as Dolores stammered and spluttered a garbled response. "W..we.. well, you see, we make a p..plastic f..formula that..." Dolores trailed off. There was no answer she could give, neither of the twins had a clue what to say.

"Next!" Mrs Smith shouted. "I've heard enough from you two."

All the color drained from Alan's face, my hands were shaking so hard I dropped all my papers, scattering them on the steps as we trooped onto the stage. Alan got busy with setting up the projector and speakers, Nicole was concentrating on stilling her shaking hands – she was responsible for the slide show and it had to be perfect.

I was mouthing my speech silently, but my heart was pounding.

"We are pleased to present our entry in the IDEA contest," Nicole began. "Tiffany will take you through the slide show now and we'll answer any questions you may have afterwards."

A scant smattering of applause followed. The lights dimmed. 'Click'- I pressed the button on the remote. An image of a dolphin filled the screen. I took a deep breath and began.

"Dolphins are mammals," I began. "Some dolphins live in the ocean and some live in rivers." I pressed another button and a fishing boat replaced the dolphin. "Today, I want to talk about the threat to these amazing creatures, something called dolphin bycatch."

The slide shows a fishing net hanging in the water. Small fish were swimming into the open net - followed by dolphins.

"When fishermen drag their nets through the water or trawl for fish, dolphins sometimes get caught in the nets," I explained.

"This is a very dangerous situation. If the dolphins can't get loose, they can drown."

The audience gasped. The slide changed, showing a dolphin tangled in the net. Trapped.

"How do we stop this happening? We have an idea," I smiled, pressing a button. The sound of whales came through the speakers.

"Those are Orcas, a natural enemy of dolphins," I explained. "The dolphins will swim away from the sound and won't get caught in the nets."

"How will your idea work?" Mrs Smith asked.

"We can design underwater speakers that play the sound of Ocras. This an affordable solution and easy to implement." I answered. Alan spent some time explaining his design of the underwater speakers.

When they had run out of questions to ask, the judges rose from their seats and began clapping. The audience joined in and this time, the applause was deafening. Turning to each other and nodding, the judges didn't take very long to announce the winners.

"We are very impressed with the standard of presentation and the originality of Dolphin Woof," Mrs Smith announced. "This invention will be very useful to the fishing industry. Tiffany, Nicole and Alan, congratulations. You are this year's winners of the Best Tech Idea contest!

Nicole, Alan and I hugged each other, jumping for joy. We'd done it! Despite the deviousness of the Frankie twins, we'd managed to turn in the winning science project. There was no sight as sweet as the sour looks on those pinched faces. The twins stormed out of the hall, slamming the door.

Ingenuity and uniqueness belong to each and every individual. They can never be stolen, or even given away. They are yours and yours alone. Don't waste or squander them - work hard, challenge yourself and never stop learning.

As for us? We take turns to host the winner's trophy and have been invited to visit the large fish market in the fall to discuss our invention. Right now, we are totally enjoying the summer vacation. We take Bailey with us to the beach every day. Because without his warning, there wouldn't be a Dolphin's Woof!

Join the

WIZKIDS CLUB

Enter today and win
a FREE BOOK!

Do you have any travel
adventure stories or project ideas
you want share with me? Yes?
Great! You can mail me at my id
and become a member of
the WIZKIDS CLUB!

www.wizkidsclub.com

Write to me at: sumita@wizkidsclub.com

Made in the USA
Middletown, DE
12 April 2019